M000278102

AFRICAN-AMERICANS

a

book

of

postcards

POMEGRANATE ARTBOOKS, SAN FRANCISCO

Pomegranate Artbooks
Box 6099
Rohnert Park, CA 94927

Pomegranate Europe Ltd.
Fullbridge House, Fullbridge
Maldon, Essex CM9 4LE
England

ISBN 0-87654-450-2
Pomegranate Catalog No. A543

Pomegranate publishes books of
postcards on a wide range of subjects.
Please write to the publisher for more information.

Designed by W. Nicholas Valentine
Printed in Korea
05 04 03 02 01 00 99   18 17 16 15 14 13 12 11 10 9

AS SCHOOLCHILDREN WE LEARNED of agricultural scientist George Washington Carver and educator Booker T. Washington, African-Americans born into slavery who went on to leave significant marks in the history of all peoples. In those same stuffy social science texts we read of slave Frederick Douglass' extraordinary escape from his "owners" to become a leading abolitionist and prominent member of the fledgling Republican Party.

Later, we learned of crusading journalist W. E. B. Du Bois, a founder of the NAACP, and Mary Bethune, innovative black educator and leader of southern and national women's organizations.

Our studies in literature led to poet and writer Langston Hughes *(Not Without Laughter)*, folklorist Nora Zeale Hurston *(Mules and Men)*, playwright Lorraine Hansberry *(A Raisin in the Sun)* and novelist Richard Wright *(Native Son)*.

Political science introduced us to clergyman and congressman Adam Clayton Powell, longtime architect of government policy on labor and education. Also springing from the pulpit into politics was Nobel Peace Prize-winning civil rights leader Martin Luther King, Jr. Black nationalist Marcus Garvey was the most influential black leader of the early 1920s, and later Malcolm X left the Black Muslims to form the Organization of Afro-American Unity, which promoted black independence and pride in the turbulent 1960s.

Our playing fields and gymnasiums produced legends like boxer Jack Johnson, in 1908 the first African-American heavyweight champion. But black athletes like Brooklyn Dodger baseball star Jackie Robinson fought racism as well as opponents on (and off) the field. Lanky Althea Gibson swept to unprecedented consecutive-year victories on the tennis courts of Wimbledon and Forest Hills (U.S. Open) in 1957–58.

Away from school we met the giants of entertainment, the African-American faces most familiar to the public. Paul Robeson, an all-American footballer in college, went on to international fame as a concert baritone and actor. Blues singer Bessie Smith was among the first so-called crossover artists whose music was heard and appreciated by white as well as black audiences. But many African-American entertainers, like cabaret singer and dancer Josephine Baker, moved to Europe to free themselves of poverty and racial oppression.

Gospel singer Mahalia Jackson and contralto Marian Anderson graced opera and concert halls throughout the world; jazz singers Billie Holiday and Lena Horne worked clubs and traveled on the road with historic big bands like that of Duke Ellington. Also in the clubs were legendary jazz instrumentalists, the most prominent of all, Charlie "Bird" Parker. Film stars Dorothy Dandridge and Harry Belafonte (better known as a popular singer) worked together in *Carmen Jones*, an adaptation of Bizet's opera. A headliner at glitzy clubs and casinos, comedian Dick Gregory used his celebrity to advance civil rights.

From faces familiar to faces less known: photographer James Van DerZee made other faces more familiar than his own with his striking portraits, and explorer Mathew Henson may have been the actual discoverer of the North Pole in 1909.

African-Americans

George Washington Carver (1864?–1943), agricultural chemist who won international acclaim for his discoveries of hundreds of uses for the peanut, sweet potato and soybean, which stimulated the cultivation of these crops and led to the diversification of the economy of the South

Pomegranate, Box 6099, Rohnert Park, CA 94927

Photograph courtesy Library of Congress

African-Americans

Booker T. Washington (1856–1915), educator and writer who organized and directed Tuskegee Institute, one of the leading African-American educational institutes in America

Pomegranate, Box 6099, Rohnert Park, CA 94927

African-Americans

Frederick Douglass (1817?–1895), abolitionist, lecturer and writer who escaped slavery in 1838, bought his freedom, and founded and edited *The North Star*, an abolitionist paper, from 1847 to 1860. Lincoln sought Douglass' counsel during the Civil War.

Pomegranate, Box 6099, Rohnert Park, CA 94927

African-Americans

Mary McLeod Bethune (1875–1955), who founded the Daytona Normal and Industrial Institute for Negro Girls, which later merged with Cookman Institute to become Bethune-Cookman College. Bethune served as special adviser on minority affairs to President Franklin Roosevelt and was the first African-American woman to hold federal office.

Pomegranate, Box 6099, Rohnert Park, CA 94927

Photograph courtesy D. C. Public Library

African-Americans

William Edward Burghardt Du Bois (1868–1963), civil rights leader and author who cofounded the National Negro Committee in 1909, which later became the NAACP

Pomegranate, Box 6099, Rohnert Park, CA 94927

Photograph courtesy Moorland-Spingarn Research Center, Howard University

African-Americans

Langston Hughes (1902–67), poet, a major figure in the Harlem Renaissance who employed African-American dialect and jazz rhythms in his poems

Pomegranate, Box 6099, Rohnert Park, CA 94927

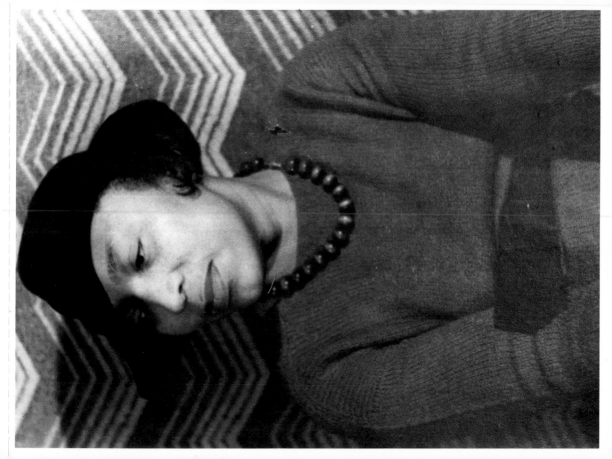

African-Americans

Zora Neale Hurston (1901?–60), writer, anthropologist and folklorist, who was the most widely published African-American woman writer of her era. Her most famous works were *Mules and Men* and *Tell My Horse*, major contributions to the knowledge of black American, African and Caribbean folklore.

Pomegranate, Box 6099, Rohnert Park, CA 94927

African-Americans

Lorraine Hansberry (1930–65), the first African-American woman to have a play on Broadway *(A Raisin in the Sun)* and the first African-American and youngest American to win the New York Drama Critics Circle Award for Best Play of the Year

Pomegranate, Box 6099, Rohnert Park, CA 94927

African-Americans

Richard Wright (1908–60), author best known for his novel *Native Son* (1940), which addressed the plight of the victimized African-American fighting against political and social conditions in Chicago in the 1930s

Pomegranate, Box 6099, Rohnert Park, CA 94927

African-Americans

Adam Clayton Powell, Jr. (1908–72), politician and clergyman, first elected to the U.S. Congress in 1945. Powell was expelled by the House of Representatives in 1967, but was overwhelmingly reelected in a special election in 1967 and again in 1968. In 1969, the U.S. Supreme Court ruled that his expulsion from the House had been unconstitutional.

Pomegranate, Box 6099, Rohnert Park, CA 94927

Photograph courtesy Michael Ochs Archives

African-Americans

Martin Luther King, Jr. (1929–68), civil rights leader who gained national promi-
nence through his advocation of passive resistance to segregation. He presented
his best known speech, ''I Have a Dream,'' at the March on Washington in 1963
to 200,000 people. He received the Nobel Peace Prize in 1964.

Pomegranate, Box 6099, Rohnert Park, CA 94927

African-Americans

Marcus Garvey (1887–1940), who founded the Universal Negro Improvement Association (1914) and was a major proponent of the ''Back to Africa'' movement; the most influential African-American leader of the early 1920s

Pomegranate, Box 6099, Rohnert Park, CA 94927

Photograph courtesy Marcus Garvey Papers, UCLA

African-Americans

Malcolm X (1925–65), prominent leader of the Black Muslim movement and, later, founder of the Organization of African-American Unity

Pomegranate, Box 6099, Rohnert Park, CA 94927

African-Americans
Jack Johnson (John Arthur Johnson, 1878–1946), the first African-American
heavyweight boxing champion (1910–15)

Pomegranate, Box 6099, Rohnert Park, CA 94927

African-Americans

Jackie Robinson (1919–72), the first African-American baseball player to play in the major leagues (Brooklyn Dodgers, 1947–56), and the first African-American to gain admission to the National Baseball Hall of Fame.

Pomegranate, Box 6099, Rohnert Park, CA 94927

African-Americans

Althea Gibson (b. 1927), tennis champion, the first African-American to win a major title (the French Championship in Paris in 1956). Gibson won Wimbledon and U.S. Open titles in 1957 and 1958, and she was the top-ranked woman player in the U.S. in 1957.

Pomegranate, Box 6099, Rohnert Park, CA 94927

African-Americans

Paul Robeson (1898–1976), film and stage actor, bass singer and political activist; graduate of Rutgers University and Columbia University law school; best known for his dramatic portrayal of the title role in *Emperor Jones* and for his interpretation of spirituals

Pomegranate, Box 6099, Rohnert Park, CA 94927

Photograph courtesy Library of Congress

African-Americans
Bessie Smith (1898?–1937), "Empress of the Blues," one of the greatest
jazz/blues singers of all time, who recorded with musicians such as Louis
Armstrong and Fletcher Henderson from 1923 to 1927

Pomegranate, Box 6099, Rohnert Park, CA 94927

African-Americans

Josephine Baker (1906–75), dancer and cabaret performer who was a dominant
figure in the nightlife of Paris in the 1920s and 1930s

Pomegranate, Box 6099, Rohnert Park, CA 94927

African-Americans

Mahalia Jackson (1911–72), gospel singer and civil rights leader who debuted at
Carnegie Hall in 1950 and who was closely associated with the work of Martin
Luther King, Jr.

Pomegranate, Box 6099, Rohnert Park, CA 94927

Photograph by Carl Van Vechten; courtesy Moorland-Spingarn Research Center,
Howard University

African-Americans
Marian Anderson (b. 1902), contralto, the first African-American to be named a permanent member of the Metropolitan Opera Company, and the first African-American to perform at the White House

Pomegranate, Box 6099, Rohnert Park, CA 94927

Photograph courtesy Moorland-Spingarn Research Center, Howard University

African-Americans

Billie Holiday (1915–59), jazz singer whose unique phrasing and highly personal interpretations of songs made her one of the most famous jazz singers of all time. Holiday ("Lady Day") performed with the bands of Count Basie, Benny Goodman and Artie Shaw before embarking on a career of solo performances in 1940.

Pomegranate, Box 6099, Rohnert Park, CA 94927

Photograph courtesy Michael Ochs Archives

African-Americans

Lena Horne (b. 1917), singer and actress whose many successes range from being the first African-American woman vocalist to be featured with a white band (Charlie Barnet's orchestra), and who at the age of 63 staged a one-woman Broadway hit *The Lady and Her Music* (1981)

Pomegranate, Box 6099, Rohnert Park, CA 94927

African-Americans

Duke (Edward Kennedy) Ellington (1899–1974), jazz musician and composer and one of the most important figures in American jazz, best known for ''Mood Indigo,'' ''Satin Doll,'' ''Take the A Train'' and many others

Pomegranate, Box 6099, Rohnert Park, CA 94927

African-Americans
Charlie ''Bird'' Parker (1920–55), composer and master of the alto saxophone
and one of the leaders of the bop movement in jazz; renowned especially for his
brilliant improvisations

Pomegranate, Box 6099, Rohnert Park, CA 94927

African-Americans

Dorothy Jean Dandridge (1922–65), the first African-American woman to be nominated for an Academy Award as best actress for her performance in *Carmen Jones* in 1954

Pomegranate, Box 6099, Rohnert Park, CA 94927

African-Americans

Harry George Belafonte (b. 1927), who gained stardom as a calypso singer with songs he made famous such as ''Day-O,'' ''Brown Skin Girl'' and ''Jamaica Farewell.'' Belafonte has been active in the civil rights movement, and he produced the first African-American TV special.

Pomegranate, Box 6099, Rohnert Park, CA 94927

African-Americans
Dick Gregory (b. 1932), comedian and political activist who was actively involved
in the civil rights and anti-Vietnam War movements in the late 1960s; shown here
in 1980 at the march for the Project 80 Coalition for Black Colleges

Pomegranate, Box 6099, Rohnert Park, CA 94927

Photograph by Julia Gaines; courtesy D. C. Public Library

African-Americans

Thurgood Marshall (1908–1993), powerful civil rights attorney and judge whose efforts helped end segregation in voting, housing, public education, and other areas, and the first African-American justice to serve on the U.S. Supreme Court

African-Americans

Matthew Alexander Henson (1866–1955), the member of Admiral Robert Peary's expedition team to the North Pole who guided Peary to the Pole, and who may have been the actual discoverer of the Pole

Pomegranate, Box 6099, Rohnert Park, CA 94927